MW01708711

The Animal Wellness

# natural cookbook *for dogs*

By Suzi Beber and the publishers of Animal Wellness Magazine

The Animal Wellness

# natural cookbook *for dogs*

By Suzi Beber and the publishers of Animal Wellness Magazine

Editorial direction: Dana Cox
Art Director & Senior Designer: Kathleen Atkinson
Senior Designer: Dawn Cumby-Dallin
Photos: Kathleen Atkinson, Dana Cox, Dawn Cumby-Dallin

All rights reserved. This material has been written and published for informational purposes only and is not meant to replace veterinary care, advice or services. It is the publisher's understanding, and the reader's, that people will act on this information at their own risk. The publisher shall have neither liability nor responsibility to any person, animal, or entity with respect to any loss, damage, or injury caused or alleged to be caused, directly or indirectly, by the contents of this book.

ISBN# 978-0-9920242-0-8

Copyright 2013 Redstone Media Group
Manufactured in China

redstone
MEDIA GROUP

Improving the lives of animals...
one reader at a time.

Join our
**AW RECIPE CLUB**
**AnimalWellnessMagazine.com/recipeclub**

Dogs are known as opportunistic omnivores. That means they'll eat pretty much anything; just ask someone with a Lab! To thrive and be as healthy as possible, however, canines need nutritious, natural food.

As the founder and editor in chief of *Animal Wellness Magazine*, I've been advocating for natural nutrition for years. In fact, every issue of *Animal Wellness* features natural nutrition tips, articles and recipes. Now we've compiled the very best information from all of our issues in this comprehensive Cookbook.

We're not saying you have to cook like this every day. But I can tell you from experience that the joy you'll get from watching your furry friend crunch down one of your homemade cookies or savor a hearty meal you prepared from scratch is priceless and so rewarding – for you and your dog!

In some cases, dogs need extra help with their diet. I've had several rescue dogs who came to me with diet-related issues. No two were the same and taking an individual approach to their nutrition needs made a world of difference to their quality of life. For these kinds of dogs, we've included a section on Special Needs, which covers a variety of conditions.

Throughout *The Animal Wellness Natural Cookbook for Dogs*, you'll find beneficial facts about the ingredients in our recipes. We're so lucky that Nature has put a wealth of nutrition at our fingertips. Now all you have to do is get it into your dog's bowl!

Happy "cooking"!

Dana Cox

P.S. For more information on all-natural products that help keep your dog in optimum health, please check out *AnimalWellnessMarket.com*.

Suzi Beber has been creating special needs diets for dogs and cats for many years, and has done extensive research into balanced home prepared diets. Following the loss of her beloved golden retriever, Blues, to cancer at only six years of age, she founded The Smiling Blue Skies Cancer Fund in 2001 through the University of Guelph's Pet Trust. Suzi has been awarded the Queen Elizabeth II Diamond Jubilee medal for her work with pets and people with cancer and is the only two-time recipient of the Golden Retriever Club of Canada's Silmaril Kennel Trophy for the Human/Animal Bond.

*The Smiling Blue Skies Cancer Fund*

A portion of all proceeds from the sale of this book will be donated to The Smiling Blue Skies Cancer Fund, which provides funding for cancer research and treatment for companion animals. One initiative, funded through The Smiling Blue Skies Fund for Innovative Research, creatively researches cancer at its most fragile and vulnerable early stage, which has important implications for human cancers too.

For more info, visit *www.smilingblueskies.com*

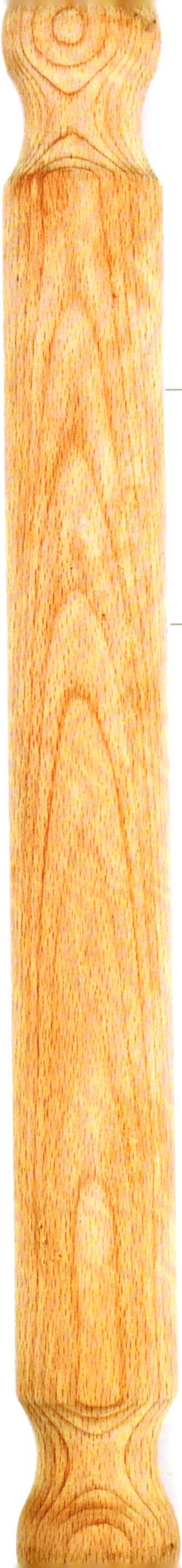

# table of contents

# getting started!

Is it possible to create a diet that's tasty, nutritious and well balanced? Absolutely!

All you need is a little bit of knowledge and some inspiration. *The Animal Wellness Natural Cookbook for Dogs* provides both! Whether you want to prepare *100%* of your dog's diet from scratch, or only experiment with treats and the occasional special meal, you'll find this book a terrific resource.

## essential information

Most holistic veterinarians agree that homemade diets top commercial products every time, provided they're prepared and balanced properly. This is very important. Fortunately, dogs generally love to eat, so this is relatively simple.

Dogs are opportunistic omnivores. You can probably relate to this – your dog will most likely take any opportunity to eat whatever he can find, whether it's meat, veggies or grains. The good news is, that makes him your biggest fan! Even if he could talk you'd never hear "Not that again!" or "Do I have to eat this?" come out of his mouth.

## pass the protein

According to the National Research Council, dogs require protein in their diets to survive. Protein contains 10 essential amino acids and high quality protein sources serve up a good balance of all of these.

## don't forget the fats and fatty acids

Dietary fats and essential fatty acids (EFAs) from fish and plant sources provide a concentrated source of energy and are important to cell structure and function. EFAs support healthy skin and coat, and fish sources help with cognitive function.

## balancing calcium and phosphorous is crucial

Dogs require 12 minerals in their diet, many of which are present in only trace amounts. Meat naturally contains phosphorous but it must be balanced with calcium, an essential building block for strong bones and teeth, in the proper phosphorous/calcium ratio. Take lots of care when choosing a pure bone meal supplement for your dog to ensure you get a quality product, and follow the dosage directions on the label. You can also make your own calcium supplement by drying organic eggshells overnight and then pulverizing them in a coffee grinder. Add 1/2 teaspoon to each pound of meat served.

**Your dog's diet also needs to include vitamins (A, D, and E) and carbohydrates for energy.**

## grains *or* no-grains?

Carbohydrates have received a lot of attention over the last few years. Some believe grains are inappropriate for our dogs, and use sweet potato instead. Others feel that high quality grains, served in moderate proportions, are a good form of energy, especially for active dogs. The recipes in this book do contain carbohydrates in one form or another. Only you can determine the optimal form for your dog. No two dogs are the same, so it's important to look at each one individually.

## veggies *and* fruits

Since dogs do not have the necessary enzymes to break down cellulose walls found in the outer layers of fruits and vegetables, we have to break the walls down for them. You can either cook or steam the vegetables or create a raw puree by putting the raw veggies in a food processor, blender, juicer or grinder. Most fruits just need a fast spin in a processor.

See page 56 for a list of top veggies and fruits, and what to avoid. For a complete breakdown of your dog's mineral and vitamin needs, visit *AnimalWellnessMagazine.com/cookbook*

## other *supplements*

Depending on your dog's needs, you can add a variety of supplements to her diet. For cooked recipes, consider adding digestive enzymes to help her absorb as much nutrition as possible from her food. Pre- and probiotics are good for a healthy intestinal tract, while a glucosamine/chondroitin sulfate supplement can help with stiff joints. Learn more at *AnimalWellnessMagazine.com*

*Filtered Water*

Like humans, all animals thrive on clean, pure water. If you can, use filtered water for your dog, too!

CAN ALSO BE SERVED RAW

## raw *vs* cooked

Another growing trend is to feed a raw diet. Many dogs can do very well on a raw diet while others may do better on cooked diets (especially those with gastro-intestinal issues or who are immune-compromised). Several of the recipes in this book can be prepared either raw or cooked. For raw, just look for the "CAN ALSO BE SERVED RAW" logo on the recipe page and follow the instructions.

## keep it *clean*

Remember, whenever you're handling raw meat, eggs and fish, it's important to wash everything in hot, soapy water afterwards, including your hands.

## is *organic* worth it?

Absolutely! Use organic meats, fruits, veggies and grains whenever possible. If it's not possible or too costly for your budget, make sure you wash the ingredients well before using. Try sourcing seasonal produce in your local area first. Farmer's markets are great for this, weather permitting.

## *how* much do I feed?

According to the NRC guidelines, an inactive 50 lb dog requires an average of 989 calories per day, while an active dog of the same weight needs approximately 1,353 calories per day. A moderately active dog would therefore require around 1,200 calories (add 1,353 and 989 and divide by 2).

For the most part, the quantities provided in this cookbook make enough food for a moderately active 50 lb. dog for one day. Dogs half the size will eat just over half, while 100 lb. dogs will consume just under double a recipe. If you're making food in bulk, keep no more than two or three days' worth of food in the fridge, and freeze the rest in serving sized containers.

*The chart below outlines the caloric needs of various sized dogs.*

### average *daily* energy needs

| | calories per day (kilocalories per day)* | | | | |
|---|---|---|---|---|---|
| type of dog | 10 lb | 30 lb | 50 lb | 70 lb | 90 lb |
| *puppies*<br>(10 lb puppy growing to 33 lb at maturity) | 990 | – | – | – | – |
| *inactive dogs*<br>Dogs with strong stimulus and ample opportunity to exercise, such as dogs in households with more than one dog, in the country or with a large yard | 296 | 674 | 989 | 1,272 | 1,540 |
| *pregnant dogs*<br>From 4 weeks after mating until delivery. | 518 | 1,274 | 1,940 | 2,570 | 3,170 |
| *young adult active dogs* | 436 | 993 | 1,451 | 1,876 | 2,264 |
| *older active dogs* | 327 | 745 | 1,093 | 1,407 | 1,700 |

*The term "calorie" used on food nutrition labels is really a "food calorie". It is equivalent to 1,000 calories (or 1 kilocalorie) as calories are defined scientifically (the amount of energy needed to warm 1 gram of water 1° C).

For a complete analysis of ingredients, including caloric content, percentage of protein, carbohydrates, fats, vitamins and minerals, based on serving size, visit the USDA database at *Nal.usda.gov/fnic/foodcomp/search.* It's comprehensive and simple to use.

Check out the

## AW Recipe Club

online for new ideas

*AnimalWellnessMagazine.com/recipeclub*

## variety is the *spice* of life!

Remember, dogs love variety too, and it helps balance out the nutrients he gets from various foods. So change up the ingredients. Mix and match, and choose from a variety of protein sources.

## switch *slowly*

If your dog has been eating a packaged commercial food his whole life, you'll want to switch him to his homemade diet over a couple of weeks. Slowly increase amounts of the new foods to his regular diet, while cutting back on the latter.

It's always a good idea, when embarking on any new diet for your dog, to work with a holistic vet, especially if your animal has a health issue.

Home preparing food for your dog might seem daunting at first, but the more you do it and the more you learn, the more you'll get into it. Best of all, your dog will reward you with better health, more energy, and a longer, happier life.

*bon appetit!*

### TOP 10 HERBS

CATNIP
DANDELION
GARLIC
GINGER
OREGANO
PARSLEY
SAGE
SLIPPERY ELM
THYME
TURMERIC

dental delights
page 26

# treats & desserts

# topsy turkey treats

*The one they'll do any trick for!*

## ingredients

2 cups "stewed" chicken or turkey (see below)

2 cloves garlic

1 tablespoon Parmesan cheese

1 tablespoon fresh Italian or curly parsley

2 eggs

2 cups whole flour of your choice (e.g., oat, barley, spelt, Red Fife, chickpea, hemp or a combination)

2 tablespoons olive oil

**Stewed Chicken Or Turkey**:
Boil the remains of a turkey or chicken carcass and scrape off all remaining meat into the broth. Besides using "sludge" for this recipe, you can also add a little bit to your dog's food just before serving, for an extra special tasty treat.

*The facts on garlic:*
Garlic offers potassium, zinc, selenium, vitamin A, vitamin B1, vitamin C, calcium, manganese, copper, and iron. It has antimicrobial properties, inhibiting the growth of bacteria and fungi. Garlic stabilizes blood pressure and supports the immune system.

## instructions

Preheat oven to 350°F. In a food processor or blender, combine the "sludge" with all the other ingredients until dough pulls away from the sides of the bowl. Turn the dough out onto a floured board or onto parchment paper and knead well – about 12 times.

Let the dough stand for about 10 minutes, then roll it out to about ½" thickness, and cut into desired shapes and sizes. You can also form the dough into small balls and pat them down with a fork on a baking sheet, try your hand at making mini pretzels, or roll out in a sheet and score with a knife or pizza cutter.

Bake for 20 minutes, then turn the oven down to 175°F and bake for 40 more minutes. Turn off oven and allow treats to get bone hard.

When the treats have completely cooled, store them in an airtight container or Ziploc bag in the refrigerator. They can also be frozen.

Note: For special occasions, remove the treats from the oven after they have been baked 20 minutes. Beat an egg white and glaze the treats, sprinkle with extra Parmesan cheese and a bit of dried parsley or oregano, and return to the oven to finish the baking process. Woof!

See photo page 20

# pup-kin cranberry muffins

*Pumpkin is not just for the holidays anymore.*

## ingredients

2 eggs

½ cup oil of your choice
(e.g. safflower, sunflower, olive, canola)

1 cup pure pumpkin puree

1½ cups whole grain flour
(e.g. oat or spelt or a combination)

1½ teaspoons cinnamon

1 teaspoon carob powder

1 teaspoon baking powder

1 teaspoon baking soda

½ teaspoon sea salt (optional)

1 cup fresh or ½ cup dried cranberries,
finely chopped

## instructions

Preheat oven to 375°F. Combine eggs, oil and pumpkin puree in a food processor or blender. Add dry ingredients and whirl together until smooth. Fold in finely chopped cranberries. Lightly grease mini muffin tins or line with paper cups, and fill each with muffin batter.

Bake for 15 minutes. Remove muffins from oven and cool completely before storing in an airtight container or Ziploc bag. This recipe can easily be doubled, and the muffins freeze beautifully.

This recipe makes approximately 34 mini muffins. For an extra special touch, the muffins can be dipped in low-fat cream cheese and decorated with cranberries and sprigs of fresh mint.

See photo page 29

*The benefits of pumpkin:*
In addition to their very high fiber content, pumpkins boast good amounts of vitamin A, most of the B vitamins, calcium, copper, magnesium, potassium, and zinc.

# hugs and *kisses* woofles

*The name says it all - you provide the most important ingredient – love!*

## ingredients

4 cups whole grain flour
(e.g. oat, spelt or a combination)

½ cup oatmeal

1 egg

2 tablespoons safflower oil

1 teaspoon carob powder

2 teaspoons cinnamon

1½ cups filtered water

## instructions

Preheat oven to 300°F. Mix all ingredients together, then turn out onto a lightly floured surface and knead well. Roll out dough to 1/8". Cut dough into shapes. Place woofles on parchment paper on cookie sheets. Bake for 55 minutes, then turn down oven to 150°F and bake for two hours. Turn the oven off. Try to leave the woofles in the oven overnight, so they are really bone hard. This way, you do not have to store them in a special container or refrigerate them.

See photo page 20

*The benefits of cinnamon:*

Cinnamon has a long history as both a spice and as a medicine. It was first used medicinally in Egypt and parts of Europe, as far back as 500 BC. In both traditional Chinese medicine and Ayurveda, cinnamon is recognized as an excellent circulation tonic.

# sweet and savory *spice* snacks

*Use whatever you have on hand to create a delicious treat. It's never the same twice!*

## ingredients

4 cups whole flour – use one whole flour or a combination of flours, e.g. whole brown rice flour (contains bran and germ), whole oat flour, whole barley flour, chickpea, potato, quinoa, tapioca, hemp or coconut flour

1 cup filling – choose from fresh fruits and vegetables and hormone-free, antibiotic-free protein sources. Try bison, chicken, turkey, venison, rabbit, fish, ostrich, emu or duck, or choose unsweetened applesauce, organic canned pumpkin, butternut squash, banana or berries. You can make a vegetable and fruit blend, like sweet potato and cranberries.

1 part spice or herb combination - consider 2 teaspoons ground cinnamon and 2 teaspoons ground carob powder for fruit based sweet treats; and 1 finely minced garlic clove and 2 teaspoons fresh parsley (or 1 teaspoon ground dried parsley) for savory treats that contain meat or fish. Here are a couple more spicy combinations to try:

- Apple pie spice: 1 tablespoon ground cinnamon, 1 teaspoon ground cloves, 1 teaspoon ground nutmeg, ½ teaspoon ground cardamom
- Pumpkin pie spice: ¼ cup ground cinnamon, 1 tablespoon ground ginger, 1 tablespoon ground nutmeg, 1 tablespoon ground cloves

## instructions

Preheat oven to 325°F. Cover a large cookie sheet with parchment paper. Combine all ingredients in a food processor until the dough pulls away from the sides of the bowl.

Turn out dough onto a lightly floured surface and knead well. Cut into desired shapes or squares and place on cookie sheet. Or take small pieces of dough and roll out to the thickness of a pencil, and using a sharp knife or pizza cutter, cut pieces appropriate to your dog's size (like mini biscotti) and place on cookie sheet. Another alternative is to form the dough into a ball, place it in the center of the cookie sheet, and using a rolling pin, roll it out to the edges and score with a sharp knife or pizza cutter.

Bake for 20 minutes, then turn oven down to 175°F and bake for 40 more minutes. Turn oven off and let biscuits cool completely in the oven, before storing them in an airtight container or Ziploc bag.

See photo page 21

*The benefits of chickpeas:*
Aka garbanzo beans, chickpeas are a source of potassium, phosphorus, iron, folate, copper, and magnesium. They contain unsaturated fatty acids and are high in fiber and protein. Best of all, the high protein content does not turn into glucose in the bloodstream.

# carob *liver* brownies

*Who doesn't love brownies? This sugar-free version uses carob instead of cocoa (a no-no for pets) and are a huge hit with the canine crowd.*

## ingredients

1 cup yogurt (without sugar or artificial sweeteners)

1 cup pureed liver (e.g. chicken, beef, ostrich)

½ cup hemp flour

1½ cups whole grain flour (e.g. spelt, oat, barley)

2/3 cups filtered water

1 teaspoon pure vanilla extract

1 teaspoon sea salt (optional)

1 tablespoon carob powder

1 teaspoon baking powder

## instructions

Preheat oven to 350°F. Lightly grease a square cake pan, or line with parchment paper. In a bowl, combine the whole oat flour and hemp seed flour with water until you have a smooth consistency. Add the yogurt and liver, and mix well. Add remaining ingredients, making sure they are all well incorporated. Pour into cake pan.

Bake for approximately 25 minutes or until the top is dry to the touch and springs back when you touch it with a finger. Cool completely before serving. Store in fridge, or cut into small squares and freeze. For extra pizzazz, ice cake with low fat cream cheese and decorate with fresh cranberries and parsley.

See photo page 20

### *The benefits of carob:*

Not only is it rich in natural sugars, carob contains all the principal minerals and vitamins, including thiamin, riboflavin, niacin, calcium, magnesium, and iron. Carob pods were used as far back as ancient Egypt as an anti-parasitic. Carob is great for calming a sick tummy, and even though it looks like cocoa, it does not contain theobromine, which can be fatal to our animal companions.

# *fantastic* flatbread

*These wholegrain treats are fun and easy to make.*

## ingredients

2 cups whole grain flour (e.g. spelt, brown rice, oat, barley or a combination)

1 cup chicken stock (or other liquid of your choice, such as beef or vegetable broth, milk, or the juice from a can of fish)

1 teaspoon sea salt (optional)

2 heaping tablespoons grated Parmesan cheese (or try liver powder, tuna, mackerel or salmon)

Extra flour for rolling dough

If you would like a softer flatbread, bake for a shorter time. For a real gourmet treat, briefly microwave the mini flatbreads before serving, and sprinkle with extra Parmesan.

*Why sea salt?*

Sea salt is an excellent source of essential minerals and trace elements.

## instructions

Preheat oven to 325°F. Place the flour and salt (if using) into a medium sized bowl. Add chicken stock or other liquid, and mix with a wooden spoon until well blended. Add the Parmesan cheese, and make sure it is well incorporated into the dough.

Turn dough out onto a clean, floured surface. Knead for two minutes, adding more flour as needed so the dough is not sticky.

Divide the dough into six balls. Roll out each into a circle about ¼" in thickness. Use lots of flour on the rolling surface and on the rolling pin, as needed.

Place the flatbread rounds on a very lightly oiled cookie sheet, and brush the tops with cold pressed olive oil. Score the surface of each flatbread with a knife or pizza slicer. Sprinkle the flatbread with poppy seeds or wheat grass.

Bake for 15 minutes, then turn the oven down to 175°F and bake for one hour more. Turn the oven off, and let the flatbreads cool completely before breaking them into bite size pieces and storing them in an airtight container or Ziploc bag.

page 16
hugs and
kisses woofles

topsy turkey treats
page 14

sweet and savory
spice snacks
page 17

page 18
carob liver brownies

page 24
c'est cheese muffins

# rise and *shine* muffins

*These healthy snacks are great in the morning or any time of day!*

## ingredients

*Dry ingredients:*

2 cups whole grain flour (e.g. oat, spelt)

2 teaspoons baking soda

2 teaspoons cinnamon

1 teaspoon carob powder

½ teaspoon sea salt (optional)

*Fruits & veggies:*

2 cups grated carrots

½ cup fresh or frozen cranberries (chopped)

½ cup unsweetened coconut

1 apple, cored and grated

*Egg mix:*

2 eggs

½ cup safflower oil, or other oil of your choice

½ cup unsweetened applesauce

## instructions

Preheat oven to 350°F. Combine the dry ingredients in a large bowl. In a separate bowl, combine the eggs, oil and applesauce. Stir this into the dry ingredients, along with the fruit and veggies. Blend so you don't see any dry spots. Spoon batter into greased mini muffin tins. Bake for 15 minutes. Remove to cooling rack, then store in a Ziploc bag in the refrigerator. Makes 24 mini muffins, or 12 to 18 with a regular sized muffin tin. These muffins freeze beautifully.

note: *Enjoy these muffins with your human family too! Replace carob with cocoa, if you wish, and add 1 cup sugar, ½ cup nuts (your choice), ½ cup raisins and 2 teaspoons vanilla.*

*Bake in a regular sized muffin pan at the same temperature for 25 minutes, or until a toothpick inserted in the center of a muffin comes out clean. Remove to cooling rack and store in Ziploc bag in the fridge. You can easily double the recipe.*

*The benefits of coconut:*
Coconut is rich in digestible oils and an excellent source of fiber.

# travel *treats*

*These treats are calming to the gastrointestinal system and contain ingredients that can help alleviate motion sickness.*

## ingredients

4 ½ cups whole oat flour

1 tablespoon cinnamon

1 tablespoon carob powder

3 cups unsweetened applesauce

1 teaspoon ginger powder

If your dog experiences motion sickness when traveling, try a 500 mg capsule of ginger, ginger snaps or crystallized ginger.

## instructions

Combine all dry ingredients in a large bowl. Add the applesauce, mixing until the dough pulls away from the sides of the bowl. If you find the mix is too wet, add extra whole oat flour or oatmeal. If it's too dry, add filtered water, a little at a time.

Line a cookie sheet with parchment paper, lightly sprinkle it with flour, then roll out the dough to a 1/4" thickness. Using a pizza cutter or sharp knife, score the dough, making the treats any size and shape you want.

Place the cookie sheet in the oven, and turn up the heat to 350°F. Once the oven reaches that temperature, turn it down to 175°F and leave the treats to slowly bake for 2 hours, or until they are bone hard.

Remove treats from the oven and cool completely before storing in a cookie jar or Ziploc bag.

See photo page 28

*The benefits of ginger:*
Ginger has long been recognized as a remedy for nausea, and helps to stimulate digestion, reducing stomach and intestinal gas and cramps.

# c'est cheese muffins

*Ooo la la! These savory muffins will be a hit with any dog who loves cheese (that would be ALL of them)!*

## ingredients

1½ cups whole grain flour of your choice (e.g. gluten-free all-purpose baking flour, a blend of whole grain flours)

2 teaspoons baking powder

½ teaspoon baking soda (gluten-free and aluminum-free)

1 tablespoon fresh or 1 teaspoon dried oregano

½ teaspoon sea salt

¼ cup first pressed extra virgin olive oil

1 cup plain goat yogurt (e.g. Greek or Balkan style)

¼ cup stock (e.g. chicken, beef, vegetable, filtered water can also be used)

1 egg

2 cups goat cheese

Oregano leaves for garnishing

## instructions

Preheat oven to 375 F. Lightly oil mini-muffin tins. Combine all ingredients in a mixer, or combine by hand using a wooden spoon or spatula. Fill each muffin cup to the top. Garnish each with an oregano leaf. Bake for 15 minutes. Muffin tops will appear golden.

Allow to cool a few minutes, then remove muffins and cool completely on a rack or plate. Store in an airtight container or Ziploc bag. Muffins must be refrigerated. They also freeze beautifully.

Makes 24 mini-muffins, but you can easily double the recipe.

See photo page 21

*The benefits of goat milk:*

Goat milk contains more vitamins B1, B2, B6, B12, biotin, folic acid, and pantothenic acid than cow's milk, and it is easier to digest due to its protein makeup. Goat's milk yogurt is the best choice for carnivores like cats, because it contains a higher percentage of fatty acids than any other milk.

# doggone *great* granola bars

*Hit the hiking trails with these energy-packed treats – perfect for you and your dog!*

## ingredients

- 1/4 cup hemp butter (or almond butter)
- 1/4 cup apple butter
- 1/3 cup unpasteurized honey
- 4 cups granola (with no added sugar or salt)
- 2 tablespoons almond meal
- 3 tablespoons hemp oil or cold-pressed vegetable oil
- 1/4 cup carob powder
- 1/2 cup unsweetened coconut
- 1/4 cup dried blueberries
- 1/4 cup dried cranberries
- 1 teaspoon cinnamon

## instructions

Heat the hemp, apple butters and honey in a large saucepan over medium heat, stirring until the mix comes to a boil. Quickly add the remaining ingredients and combine well.

Turn out mixture into a greased 9"x13" Pyrex dish, flatten with a spatula, and cut into squares using a sharp knife.

Cool completely. To speed the process, put the dish in the fridge. Wrap squares in waxed paper. For freezing, wrap once more in tinfoil or saran wrap. Granola bars are perfect, when you're on the road or hiking the trails with your dog. You'll enjoy them too!

As an alternative, make crunchy granola you can munch any time and share with your dog. Simply line a cookie sheet with parchment paper, turn out your granola mixture onto the cookie sheet, and place it in a preheated 200°F oven for one hour.

*The benefits of blueberries:*

Scientists have discovered that blueberries contain significant levels of resveratol, a natural compound found to have anti-cancer qualities. Blueberries are mini powerhouses of antioxidants, which come from anthocyanins, the pigments that give blueberries their deep blue shade. Like cranberries, blueberries also help to prevent urinary tract infections because they contain condensed tannins, the compounds responsible for keeping bacteria from attaching to the wall of the bladder.

# dental *delights*

*These crunchy treats are a good workout for the chompers.*

## ingredients

2 cups cooked chicken giblets
(hearts, livers, gizzards)

1 clove garlic

1 tablespoon dried oregano

1 tablespoon fresh parsley

1 tablespoon oil (e.g. olive, hemp)

1 egg

1½ cups whole grain flour
(e.g. oat, spelt, hemp or quinoa)

¼ cup dried cranberries, finely minced

Topping:

1 egg white

Parmesan cheese

*The benefits of parmesan cheese:*
Parmesan cheese is a low-lactose food and is very versatile. It is a source of calcium and phosphorus, along with other vitamins and minerals, and is the perfect sprinkle when you have a picky eater.

## instructions

Place chicken giblets in a pot and cover with filtered water. Bring the water to a boil, then turn down to simmer for 20 minutes. Preheat oven to 350°F. Cover two cookie sheets with parchment paper. In a food processor or blender, combine all ingredients except the flour, egg white and Parmesan.

Blend until you have a thick paste. Add the flour slowly, so it's well incorporated into the paste. Add a bit more oil or filtered water if your dough is too dry, or add a bit more flour if you find it's too wet.

Dust your hands with flour and sprinkle it on a board or countertop. You can use oatmeal in place of flour. Knead the dough well, then roll it out to about ¼" in thickness. This part is particularly easy if you roll out the dough on a piece of floured wax paper or parchment paper. Cut the dough into desired shapes and sizes, or take small piece of dough, roll out to the thickness of a pencil, and cut into small treats, like biscotti.

Bake for 30 minutes. Turn the oven down to 200°F and remove the cookie sheets from the oven. Beat or whisk the egg white until soft peaks begin to form. Baste the biscuits with the egg white, then liberally sprinkle them with Parmesan cheese. Return the biscuits to the oven and bake for another 45 minutes. Turn the oven off and leave the biscuits until they are completely cooled.

This recipe yields more than 50 medium sized biscuits. It can easily be doubled. The biscuits store well in the fridge and also freeze well.

note: *for small dogs, roll the dough to 1/8" thickness and cut baking time in half.*



See photo page 12

# bison and sweet potato crunch

*Cinnamon and carob add delicious flavor to these gluten free treats.*

## ingredients

1 pound bison liver

1/2 cup grated sweet potato or yam

1 teaspoon carob powder

1 teaspoon cinnamon

1/2 cup whole brown rice flour

## instructions

Preheat oven to 200°F. Combine all ingredients in a food processor or blender until smooth. Line a cookie sheet with parchment paper. Pour paste onto parchment paper. Spread with a spatula.

Place cookie sheet on middle rack of oven and bake for three hours. Take a sample and break it. You should hear a great "snap."

Cool completely before storage. This step is essential! Store in an airtight container or Ziploc bag.

*The benefits of brown rice:*

Brown rice is higher in fiber, vitamins, and minerals than white rice, and is also gluten free. It is a source of potassium, protein, iron, thiamin, and niacin.

page 23
travel treats

billie's bars
page 30

pup-kin muffins
page 15

# billie's bars

*This recipe was developed for a golden retriever named Billie, who was competing in the National Obedience Invitational.*

## ingredients

4 cups large flake oats

2 cups oatmeal

1 tablespoon carob powder

1/4 cup sunflower oil (or other oil of your choice)

2 tablespoons molasses

4 tablespoons unpasteurized honey

1 teaspoon Manuka honey

4 eggs

1 cup dried or 1½ cups fresh cranberries

1 cup boiling filtered water

## instructions

Preheat oven to 350°F. Line a 9″x12″ baking dish or cookie sheet with parchment paper.

Combine all ingredients in a large mixing bowl, except the boiling water. Add the water a little at a time, and continue to blend ingredients until all the water has been absorbed.

Spoon mixture into baking dish or onto cookie sheet, and press down with the back of a wooden spoon until the surface is even. This will make scoring easier after baking.

Bake for 45 minutes. Remove from oven and score into bars, using a sharp knife. Cool completely before storing in an airtight container or a Ziploc bag.

See photo page 29

*The benefits of oats:*

In addition to a high silicon content, which makes them beneficial to bones and connective tissues, oats are known to soothe the digestive and nervous systems. They are high in mineral content, particularly potassium and phosphorus, and contain calcium, magnesium, vitamin B, and provide a good source of iron. On top of all this, oats help to cleanse the intestines of impurities.

# liver and honey *energy* drops

*These frozen treats make a great pick-me-up and they're so simple to make! You can buy hemp hearts at the health food store.*

## ingredients

1/2 pound raw chicken livers

2 tablespoons unpasteurized honey

Hemp hearts

## instructions

Whirl chicken livers and honey in a food processor or blender until smooth. Add hemp hearts until the mixture just begins to pull away from the sides of the bowl.

Form small balls, roll in extra hemp hearts, gently flatten with a fork, and freeze on a cookie sheet covered with parchment paper.

When frozen, drops can be transferred to an airtight container or Ziploc bag.

*The benefits of honey:*

Honey is packed with antioxidants and flavonoids, but make sure to buy unpasteurized for maximum effect.

# bison burger bits

*Herbs, cheese, fruit... this treat has it all!*

## ingredients

1 pound ground bison

2 cups whole grain flour of your choice, or try sweet potato flour

1 tablespoon dried or 2 heaping tablespoons fresh oregano, finely minced

1 tablespoon dried marjoram

1 teaspoon sea salt

2 tablespoons Parmesan cheese

Dash of cayenne

3 heaping tablespoons fresh Italian parsley leaves, finely minced

2 cloves garlic, finely minced

1 egg

1 tomato, minced

¼ cup beef or vegetable broth, or filtered water

Fresh or dried blueberries and cranberries

## instructions

Line a cookie sheet with parchment paper and preheat oven to 350°F. Combine all ingredients in a food processor or blender. Take small pieces of dough and form small balls, roll them lightly in rolled oats, place on cookie sheet and lightly flatten using your "fingerprint" – the perfect size for holding a blueberry or cranberry. A teaspoon makes perfectly sized bits.

Bake 30 to 35 minutes. Remove from oven and transfer bits to a plate that can be put in the fridge to cool. Store in the freezer in a Ziploc bag until you are ready to defrost, warm and serve. This recipe makes 63 treats and can be easily doubled.

*The benefits of tomatoes:*

The secret to the tomato's success is lycopene, the chemical that gives tomatoes their bright red colour. Cooked tomatoes actually contain more lycopene because cooking breaks down their cellular walls, allowing carotenoids to be more concentrated. Lycopene has been found to be as effective as statins for artery health, helping to reduce plaque formation in the arteries that can cause atherosclerosis.

# peanut butter truffles

*What dog doesn't love peanut butter?*

## ingredients

1 cup peanut butter (with no added salt or sugar)
You can also use other nut or seed butters

1 cup oatmeal

½ cup carob powder

½ cup goat milk

Oatmeal for rolling

Unsweetened coconut for rolling

## instructions

Line a cookie sheet with parchment paper. Combine peanut butter, oatmeal and carob powder. Form into small balls. Lightly dip in goat milk and roll in oatmeal or coconut, and place on cookie sheet.

Place in refrigerator until serving. For extra flair, top each truffle with a sun dried cranberry. The truffles freeze beautifully in Ziploc bags.

See photo page 36

*A note about peanut butter:*

Always choose peanut butter that contains no added salt or sugar. It contains 13% carbohydrates, 72% fats, and 15% protein. Do not use peanut butter if someone in your home has an allergy to it. Instead try almond butter, hempseed butter or tahini, a seed butter made from sesame seeds.

# "apple of my eye" *fruit* crisp

*Your dog will love this seasonal favorite as much as you do!*

## ingredients

4 red apples, chopped

½ cup pure fruit juice
(e.g., apple, cranberry, mango)

2 tablespoons blueberry oil*

2 tablespoons cranberry oil*

2 tablespoons unpasteurized honey

¼ cup whole oat flakes

1 tablespoon whole blueberry flour**

1 tablespoon whole cranberry flour**

1 tablespoon dried cranberries, finely sliced or chopped

2 teaspoons cinnamon

1 tablespoon Brazil nuts, finely ground (optional)

*If unavailable in your area, fruit oils can be replaced with other oils such as hemp, rice bran, almond, etc.

**If unavailable in your area, fruit flours can be replaced with another whole flour of your choice, such as oat or spelt flour.

## instructions

Preheat oven to 350°F. Combine all ingredients in a Pyrex baking dish. Bake for 1 hour. Cool and store in the refrigerator. Fruit crisp freezes well too.

Top with goat milk yogurt for an extra special taste sensation.

*A note about fruit flours:*
These are a great alternative for gluten free diets. They are a good source of fiber and contain antioxidants, just like whole fruits, with no added sugar or preservatives.

# b-good muffins

*These muffins pack a healthy punch of B vitamins.*

## ingredients

1½ cups whole grain flour
(e.g. oat, barley, spelt)

2 teaspoons baking powder

½ teaspoon baking soda

½ teaspoon sea salt

¼ cup oil
(e.g. safflower, sunflower, hemp, olive)

¼ cup liver broth

¼ cup pureed chicken or beef liver

1 cup yogurt
(without sugar or artificial sweeteners)

1 egg

## instructions

Preheat oven to 375°F. Combine dry ingredients in a large bowl. Whirl all other ingredients in a food processor or blender.

Add wet ingredients to dry, and mix thoroughly. Spoon into lightly greased mini muffin tins and bake for 15 minutes. Remove from oven and turn out onto baking rack to cool completely. Store in an airtight container or Ziploc bag. Keep a few in the fridge and freeze the rest.

*The benefits of spelt:*
Spelt is a member of the wheat family, but it is an ancient grain. It is an excellent source of manganese and is also a good source of protein, copper, zinc, and insoluble fiber.

page 41
easier-than-pie
baked granola apple

peanut butter truffles
page 33

kelp kandy
page 38

page 43

# sweet potato and honey crisps

# kelp kandy

*The perfect combination of sweet and salty, these seaweed treats are great for training.*

## ingredients

Package of kombu (dried kelp)

1/4 cup unpasteurized honey

1/2 cup filtered water

1 cup almonds or Brazil nuts, finely ground

## instructions

Soak dried kombu pieces in filtered water until soft. Drain and, using scissors, cut into small pieces, enough to fill 1/2 cup. Combine honey with filtered water and bring to a boil. Reduce heat to simmer, add kombu, and continue to gently cook until liquid has evaporated. This takes about one hour.

Preheat oven to 300°F. Spread ground almonds or Brazil nuts on a parchment-covered cookie sheet and coat the kombu pieces in the ground nuts. Bake for 30 minutes. Cool completely before serving. The whole family can share this special treat!.

See photo page 36

*The benefits of kelp:*
Kelp promotes glandular health, especially the thyroid, pituitary and adrenal glands, as well as cardiovascular health. Kelp is also high in trace minerals and is a rich source of natural iodine.

# bountiful *buddy* bars

*Packed with seeds and fruit, these tasty bars will get his attention every time!*

## ingredients

3 cups large flake oats

1 cup oatmeal

1 cup rice cereal

1/2 cup tapioca flour

1/4 cup sunflower seeds, finely ground

1/4 cup pumpkin seeds, finely ground

1 cup fresh or frozen cranberries, finely chopped

1 tablespoon unsweetened coconut

1 heaping tablespoon cinnamon

1 teaspoon pure vanilla extract

1/2 cup boiling filtered water

1/2 cup yogurt (without sugar or artificial sweeteners)

1 teaspoon Manuka honey

4 tablespoons unpasteurized honey

1/4 cup hemp oil or another oil of your choice

## instructions

Preheat oven to 350°F. Pulse oak flakes two or three times in a food processor. Combine all ingredients in a large bowl. Spread out mixture on a cookie sheet that has been lightly oiled or lined with parchment paper. Lightly score the bars before baking.

Bake for 45 minutes. Remove cookie sheet from oven, allow bars to cool for 15 minutes, then lightly score them again. Let the bars cool completely before storing them in an airtight container or Ziploc bag in the fridge. They also freeze well.

### *The benefits of pumpkin seeds:*

Pumpkin seeds contain vitamin E, selenium (an antioxidant) and L-tryptophan, an amino acid that is responsible for the production of serotonin. They also contain glutamate, which supports the synthesis of GAGA, an anti-stress neurochemical..

# carob *cranberry* truffles

*These lovely treats are great for gift-giving. Your friends' dogs will love you!*

## ingredients

½ cup unsweetened granola

2 tablespoons carob powder

½ cup fresh or ¼ cup dried cranberries, finely chopped

3½ cups whole oat flour

½ cup pure cranberry juice

1½ cups filtered water

Goat milk or goat milk yogurt

Extra granola or oatmeal, for rolling

## instructions

Preheat oven to 325°F. Combine all ingredients, except the extra granola and milk. Form small balls the size of truffles, dip in milk or yogurt, then roll in granola or oatmeal.

Place truffles on an ungreased or parchment paper covered cookie sheet and bake for 20 minutes. Turn off oven, and allow truffles to cool completely before storing them in an airtight container.

These tempting treats freeze beautifully.
For gift giving, pop truffles into candy cups.
Then place in gift boxes or seasonal tins.

*The benefits of cranberries:*

Cranberries are mini-powerhouses of antioxidants and contain numerous biologically active compounds, including flavonoids, phenolic acids, anthocyanins and condensed tannins. Research has shown that pure cranberry juice may be just as powerful for fighting cavities as it is for bladder infections.

# easier-than-pie baked *granola* apples

*Baked apples were a special childhood dessert. This dog-friendly recipe skips the sugar but is still wonderfully tasty!*

## ingredients

4 red apples

¾ cup granola, w th no added salt or sugar

Sprinkling of cinnamon and carob

## instructions

Preheat oven to 350°F. Hollow out unpeeled apples. Fill each with granola, packing it in as tightly as you can. Place the apples in a shallow Pyrex baking dish, and sprinkle with cinnamon and carob.

Bake for 30 minutes or until apples are tender. Remove from oven and let the apples cool to room temperature. Serve plain, or add a dollop of goat milk yogurt or Balkan style yogurt.

See photo page 36

*The benefits of apples:*

Red apples are rich in antioxidants. They are heart smart and studies are even showing that a diet rich in red apples helps in our bcttle against cancer, by inhibiting the growth of cancer cells. Red apples, along with other colourful fruits and vegetables, contain the phytochemicals, lycopene and anthocyanins. Along with lots of vitamin C, red apples contain ca cium, chlorine, fluorine, iron, magnesium, phosphorus, potassium, silicon, sodium, and sulphur, and also many trace minerals.

# carob zucchini mini muffins

*Even people who don't like zucchini love zucchini bread or muffins. This dog-friendly sugar-free version is so delicious, he'll never know it's nutritious.*

## ingredients

2 eggs

1 cup yogurt (without sugar or artificial sweeteners)

½ cup safflower oil (or other oil of your choice)

2 cups grated zucchini (or carrots or apples, on their own or in combination)

½ cup dried cranberries

3 cups whole grain flour (e.g. oat, spelt)

½ cup carob powder

½ cup Brazil nuts, finely ground

½ teaspoon cinnamon

½ teaspoon ginger

½ teaspoon sea salt

1 teaspoon baking powder

1 teaspoon baking soda

## instructions

Preheat oven to 350°F. Combine eggs, yogurt, safflower oil and grated zucchini. Fold in cranberries. Combine all dry ingredients, then add to wet ingredients and mix until thoroughly blended. Lightly grease mini muffin tins, and fill each cup almost to the top.

Bake for 20 minutes. Let muffins cool completely and store in an airtight container or a Ziploc bag in the fridge.

This recipe makes 48 or more mini muffins. Muffins and dough freeze beautifully, and you can cut the recipe in half.

For a gluten free treat, try quinoa or brown rice whole grain flours.

*The benefits of zucchini:*

Zucchini is a great source of dietary fiber and is rich in vitamins A and C, both important antioxidants, as well as potassium and folate.

# sweet potato and honey crisps

*These are so delicious you'll want to share them with your whole family!*

## ingredients

3 sweet potatoes (about 1 pound), thinly sliced

¼ cup cold extracted extra virgin olive oil

1½ teaspoons local honey

1 tablespoon (or more to taste) of seasoning blend (e.g. organic dulse with garlic, Herbés de Provence, cinnamon and carob)

## instructions

Preheat oven to 425°F. Line two cookie sheets with parchment paper.

Baste sweet potatoes with olive oil and honey blend. Gently warming the oil and honey first will make basting very easy. Sprinkle potatoes with selected seasoning blend.

Bake for 15 minutes, then take the cookie sheets out of the oven, gently turn over the sweet potatoes, sprinkle with a little extra seasoning, and return to the oven for another 15 minutes.

Transfer sweet potatoes to a plate lined with a paper towel, let them cool completely, then store in an airtight container in the fridge. (That is, if they last that long - I won't tell you how many of ours disappear before they even find their way to a plate!)

note: *For extra crispy treats, let the oven cool to 250°F, then return them to the oven for a further 20 minutes, checking regularly to ensure they don't burn. Store as above.*

See photo page 37

### The benefits of sweet potato:

Sweet potatoes are very rich in antioxidants, and they are also referred to as an "anti-diabetic food" because recent research has demonstrated that sweet potatoes can help to stabilize blood sugar levels and lower insulin resistance. They also have anti-inflammatory properties and are soothing to the digestive tract. Sweet potatoes contain vitamin A, in the form of betacarotene, vitamin C, vitamin B-6, vitamin E, copper, dietary fiber, iron, manganese, and potassium.

page 46
turkey and sweet potato savory loaf

# main meals

# turkey and sweet potato *savory* loaf

*This colorful loaf tastes as good as it looks!*

## ingredients

1 pound ground turkey

1 cup shredded sweet potatoes or yams

1 egg, lightly beaten

½ cup fresh parsley, finely chopped

½ cup fresh cranberries, finely chopped

1 clove garlic, finely minced or grated

1 teaspoon sea salt

1 cup chicken or vegetable stock

Calcium, as per label instructions

## instructions

Preheat oven to 350°F. Lightly grease a loaf pan and line it with shredded sweet potatoes or yams. Lightly sprinkle minced garlic on top.

Add ½ cup of stock. Pour lightly beaten egg on top. Sprinkle 1/4 cup of parsley over the mixture, then add ¼ cup of cranberries. Distribute ground turkey evenly over mixture. Add the remaining ½ cup of stock. Sprinkle sea salt overtop. Add the remaining parsley and cranberries.

Gently press down mixture with a spatula. Bake for one hour. Cool completely before slicing and serving. Add calcium and don't forget to garnish!

Replace shredded sweet potatoes or yams with cooked and mashed. Mix together all ingredients.

See photo page 44

CAN ALSO BE SERVED RAW

*Mix together all ingredients. Alternatively, replace shredded sweet potatoes or yams with cooked and mashed.*

*The benefits of parsley:*

Parsley is rich in iron and vitamin C, and contains pro-vitamin A. Add calcium, phosphorus, and manganese to the mix, and you can see why parsley is considered one of the most concentrated food sources.

# coconut curry cake with *wild* salmon

*It sounds fancy but it's so easy to make!*

## ingredients

4 cups coconut flour

4 cups filtered water

1/3 cup olive oil

2 eggs

2 tins (7.5-ounce) wild salmon, with bones

1 teaspoon turmeric

1 teaspoon garlic

1 teaspoon ginger

Dried cranberries, finely minced

Sea salt

Acadian sea kelp

## instructions

Preheat oven to 350°F. Lightly grease two cookie sheets with olive oil. Combine all ingredients in a mixer or blender. This recipe also whips up easily by hand. Split the mixture between the two cookie sheets then pat down so the dough has a flat surface. Gently score with a pizza cutter or sharp knife.

Bake for 20 to 25 minutes. Look for golden edges. Let the cakes cool completely before removing from cookie sheets. Be extra careful as these cakes are like the finest holiday shortbreads – use a spatula. Before serving, sprinkle with cranberries, sea salt and kelp.

These cakes freeze well and also store well in containers. The recipe can easily be split in half and coconut flour used in combination with other flours.

*tasty tip*

To make your own coconut flour, just put unsweetened coconut in a food processor or blender and away you go!

See photo page 52

*The benefits of turmeric:*

Turmeric is a member of the ginger family and it contains a mix of phenolics called curcurmin. The rhizome of turmeric is used as an antioxidant and anti-inflammatory. It's a good choice for liver conditions, IBS, and other gastrointestinal problems. Turmeric is an antimicrobial and anti-carcinogen that is used for cardiovascular ailments. The positive cardiovascular effects of turmeric include lower cholesterol levels.

# sumptuous stew

*This lovely, autumn stew is perfect any time of the year.*

## ingredients

1 pound turkey, beef or lamb, ground or cut in small chunks

¼ ounce beef liver

4 cups sweet potato, chopped (or use one of the following: 4 cups white potato, ⅔ cup whole brown rice or whole white rice, 1½ cups oatmeal, ⅔ cup pearled barley or barley flakes, or ⅔ cup quinoa)

½ cup zucchini, chopped (or other green vegetable, such as green beans or broccoli)

1 clove garlic, minced

1 small red apple with skin, chopped (or ¼ cup other brightly colored fruits and berries, such as blueberries or cranberries)

Pinch of sea salt

Sprinkle of turmeric

4 cups filtered water

Calcium, as per label instructions

## instructions

Combine all ingredients in a crock pot. Cover and cook on low for six to eight hours, or on high for three to four hours. If you don't have a crock pot, simply combine all the ingredients in a big pot, bring to a gentle boil, then turn down to simmer for two to three hours, stirring from time to time so ingredients don't stick to the bottom. Add calcium before serving.

This recipe makes one day's food for a moderately active 50-pound dog. It provides approximately 1,200 calories, which includes about 30% protein, 40% carbohydrates and 30% fat.

CAN ALSO BE SERVED RAW

*Purée the veggies, cook the grains (if using) and mix all ingredients with the raw meat. Serve.*

*The benefits of barley:*

Barley has been cultivated for over 10,000 years and is considered one of the world's healthiest foods. It supports the intestines, stomach, spleen, pancreas, kidneys, thyroid, and the immune system. It's an excellent source of fiber, and selenium, which has been shown to inhibit the proliferation of cancer cells. As a co-factor of glutathione peroxidase, selenium also works alongside vitamin E, to be cardio-protective and even lessen the signs of arthritis.

sumptuous stew

# jazzy jambalaya

*Jazz up his bowl with this doggie version of a classic Creole dish.*

## ingredients

2 pounds ground meat (e.g., bison, turkey)

1/4 to 1/2 cup liver, minced

1 cup Thai jasmine rice, organic brown rice flakes, or finely grated sweet potato

3 cups stock of your choice

2 cups vegetable and fruit pureé (e.g., green beans, celery, zucchini, carrots, blueberries, cranberries)

1 cup tomato pureé

1 large fresh Shiitake mushroom, chopped

1 clove garlic, finely minced

1 teaspoon sea salt and kelp

1 teaspoon turmeric

1 teaspoon cinnamon

1/4 cup olive oil

Calcium, as per label instructions

## instructions

Bring stock to a boil in a large pot. Add rice, gently stirring to avoid sticking, turn heat down to simmer, cover the pot and leave for 5 minutes. Add remaining ingredients (except for olive oil and calcium), combine thoroughly, bring heat back up to a gentle boil, then cover the pot and turn the heat back down to a simmer for 40 minutes. Add olive oil and calcium, and mix thoroughly.

Cool, then transfer to containers for storage in the fridge or freezer. Your dog will love a fresh sprinkling of parsley before serving.

See photo page 61

CAN ALSO BE SERVED RAW

*Blend all other ingredients with cooked rice (if using) or grated sweet potato.*

*The benefits of green beans:*

Green beans are an excellent source of vitamin A. They also contain vitamins C and K, calcium, copper, fiber, folic acid, iron, magnesium, niacin, potassium, riboflavin, thiamin and Omega 3 fatty acids.

# frittini egg loaf

*This recipe is so easy to "whip" up and so versatile. Use a loaf pan or individual ramekins for special occasions.*

## ingredients

1 cup zucchini, finely chopped

1 clove garlic, finely minced or grated

5 eggs

2 tablespoons olive oil

1½ tablespoons fresh or 1 teaspoon dried oregano

2 teaspoons fresh or 1 teaspoon dried thyme

½ teaspoon sea salt

Calcium, as per label instructions

## instructions

Preheat oven to 350°F. In oven-to-table cookware, combine all ingredients with a whisk or fork. Bake for 20 minutes or until the center of the loaf is set and the top is golden. Cool to room temperature.

Before serving, garnish with fresh sunflower sprouts and parsley if you wish. Egg loaves can be made with a variety of vegetables, including 2 cups of young "greens" (includirg dandelion greens). In a pinch, a can of butternut squash is the perfect filler.

See photo page 52

CAN ALSO BE SERVED RAW

*Blend together all ingredients. Pour into dish. Eggs can be served completly raw or you can boil them in the shell for one minute.*

*The benefits of eggs:*
Eggs are the most bioavailable protein. They contain lutein, which helps to keep our dogs' skin well hydrated and plays an important role in tissue repair. The zinc found in eggs supports healthy skin and coat. Egg yolks provide a valuable source of biotin, along with vitamin E, and Omega 3 and 6 fatty acids.

page 47
coconut curry cake
with wild salmon

frittini egg loaf
page 51

page 55

# sassy *shiitake* sauté

*Mushroom lovers will really appreciate this one – a taste sensation for you and your dog.*

## ingredients

1 cup fresh Shiitake mushrooms (or other culinary mushroom of your choice), finely chopped or sliced

1 clove garlic, finely minced

1/2 teaspoon sea salt

1 tablespoon olive oil

3 cups cooked whole brown rice, Thai jasmine rice or quinoa*

1 pound of selected protein (e.g., turkey, chicken, beef, bison, lamb)

Calcium, as per label instructions

note: **To prepare quinoa, wash under cold water, using a strainer. Add 1 cup of quinoa to 1¼ cups of boiling filtered water. Reduce the heat and simmer for 15 minutes. Remove pot from stove, allow to sit for five minutes, then plump up quinoa with a fork. Cool before serving.*

## instructions

Heat oil in a large pan. Add mushrooms and garlic, and gently sauté until tender. Add rice or quinoa and salt and combine well.

Mix:
2/3 cup of the rice mixture, along with 1 pound of cooked or raw (dogs only) protein (e.g., ground turkey) This will feed a 50-pound moderately active dog for a day. This recipe is not intended to be fed every day.

See photo page 60

CAN ALSO BE SERVED RAW

*Blend either sauteed or raw mushrooms with cooked rice or quinoa and raw meat of your choice.*

*The benefits of shiitake mushrooms:*

Shiitake is truly medicine in a mushroom. Shiitake mushrooms contain a natural source of interferon, a protein that appears to induce immune response against cancer and viral diseases. The eritadenine found in Shiitake mushooms helps to decrease fat and cholesterol in the blood, and their germanium supports cellular oxygenation and the immune response. They contain more than 50 enzymes, including pepsin, which aids digestion.

# simple salmon loaf

*A great alternative to meat loaf!*

## ingredients

1 15-ounce can wild salmon, with bones

3 eggs

1 cup yogurt (without sugar or artificial sweeteners)

3/4 to 1 cup oatmeal

Flat or curly parsley for garnish

## instructions

Preheat oven to 350°F. Combine all ingredients in a food processor or blender. Turn out into a lightly greased loaf pan or Pyrex pan. Bake for 45 minutes.

Cool loaf completely before slicing and storing in refrigerator or freezer. Garnish with fresh parsley before serving. This loaf is nice for brunch.

See photo page 53

*The benefits of salmon:*
Cold water fish, like salmon, is rich in Omega-3 essential fatty acids.

# dream dinner menu options

*This sample recipe is based on National Research Council Canada guidelines and contains 30% protein, 40% carbohydrates, and 30% fat. It makes enough food for a moderately active 50-pound dog for one day.*

## ingredients

### Protein

Choose from one of the following. The meats can be ground or whole, chopped in pieces.

1½ cups chicken

1½ cups turkey

1½ cups duck

1½ cups lean beef

1½ cups bison/buffalo

1½ cups lamb (lean cuts)

1½ cups venison

1½ cups emu

1½ cups ostrich

1½ cups rabbit

1½ cups salmon

1½ cups tuna

1½ cups pollock

1½ cups mackerel

4 hard boiled eggs

### Fats

Fats are the most concentrated source of energy in the diet plan. Add a tablespoon of one of the following oils to the diet. Use cold pressed oils wherever possible.

| | |
|---|---|
| safflower | hemp seed |
| sunflower | avocado |
| canola | olive |
| grape seed | rice bran |

### Carbohydrates

Choose one carbohydrate from the list. One cup of a dry whole grain is cooked in three cups of filtered water.

3 cups of whole brown rice

3 cups of pearl barley

4½ cups of oatmeal, made from whole oats

3 cups of sweet potatoes

### Veggies and Fruits

Add ¼ cup to ½ cup of a vegetable and fruit mash that includes orange and green vegetables and brightly colored fruits.

| | |
|---|---|
| Red apples | Carrots |
| Avocados | Green beans |
| Bananas | Papaya |
| Blueberries | Pumpkin |
| Cantaloupe | Sweet potato |
| Cranberries | Tomatoes |
| Broccoli | |

Since dogs and cats do not have the necessary enzymes to break down the outer layers of fruits and vegetables, we have to do it for them so these power-packed foods can be made as bioavailable as possible.

Cooking and steaming vegetables will do the trick. Alternatively, a food processor, blender, juicer or grinder can quickly create a wonderful pureé. Most fruits just need a fast spin in a processor.

### Calcium

Use the eggshell recipe on page 8 or a calcium product. Follow the instructions on the label.

CAN ALSO BE SERVED RAW

*Blend raw meat (not fish) with cooked carbohydrates or raw grated sweet potato and puréed fruits and veggies.*

## instructions

When preparing whole grains, use 1 cup of grain and 3 cups of filtered water. For brown rice flakes, boil 3/4 cup of filtered water, add 1/2 cup of rice flakes, stir, then cook for 3 minutes.

Let your carbohydrate choice cool after preparation, add your selected protein source, some pureéd fruits and vegetables, 1 tablespoon of cold pressed vegetable oil, and that's it!

Grains or no grains: *Some dogs do well with no grains while others require them for extra energy and/or better health.*

*If you are feeding your dog a grain-free diet, try quinoa. To prepare, wash under cold water in a strainer. Add 1 cup quinoa to 1 1/4 cups of boiling filtered water. Reduce the heat and simmer for 15 minutes. Remove pot from the stove, leave it to sit for 5 minutes, then plump up the quinoa with a fork. Cool before serving.*

### *Tips for Travel*

Rice flakes are the perfect choice when you're traveling with your dog. They won't get stopped at the border and they are easy to prepare.

Canned sweet potato makes meal preparation simple when on the road. Sweet potatoes are an excellent source of vitamin E. They also provide many other nutrients, including vitamins A, B6 and C, calcium, iron, folate, potassium, copper, thiamine and iron. Sweet potatoes are a complex carbohydrate, rich in beta carotene, which may be a factor in reducing the risk of some cancers. They are also a rich source of dietary fiber and help promote a healthy gastrointestinal system.

# baked fish *cakes*

*These individual cakes pack a healthy punch and are perfect for freezing.*

## ingredients

2 pounds ground white fish

3 eggs

2 carrots

2 teaspoons sea salt (optional)

4 tablespoons oatmeal

1/4 cup oil of your choice

3/4 cup filtered water (for extra punch, use fish or vegetable stock to replace some or all of the filtered water)

Fresh or dried parsley for garnish

Calcium, as per label instructions

## instructions

Preheat oven to 350°F. Combine all ingredients, except the fish, in a food processor or blender. Turn out into a large mixing bowl. Add fish and combine thoroughly.

Line cookie sheets with parchment paper or lightly grease them.

You can make perfect large patties for your canine companion by using an old-fashioned ice cream scoop. After scooping, lightly flatten the cakes with a fork before popping them in the oven.

Bake for approximately one hour. Remove from the oven and cool completely before storing in your refrigerator or freezer. Garnish with parsley before serving.

See photo page 61

*The benefits of white fish:*

White fish is a great choice for dogs who need to lose a little weight and it is also worth considering as part of an elimination diet. It is a valuable source of vitamins and minerals, including vitamins B6 and B12.

# liver licks sauté

*Rich in iron, this dish will have them licking their lips in anticipation.*

## ingredients

½ cup raw liver, chopped

2 tablespoons filtered water

1 tablespoon potato flour

1 clove garlic, finely minced

½ teaspoon turmeric

Calcium, as per label instructions

## instructions

Combine all ingredients in a small cast iron pan. Gently sauté on medium heat. This recipe takes less than five minutes to prepare, but make sure it has cooled right down before serving.

*The benefits of potato flour:*

Great for gluten free recipes, potato flour is made from the whole potato, not simply potato starch. Potato flour is a good source of protein and fiber, along with a variety of vitamins and minerals, including vitamin B6, vitamin C, potassium and calcium.

page 5

# sassy shiitake sautee

page 50
jazzy jambalaya

baked fish cakes
page 58

# fresh and friendly *frittata*

*This convenient one-dish recipe is proof that eggs are perfect at any meal.*

## ingredients

¾ cup artichoke hearts, finely chopped (use artichokes canned in water)

1 clove garlic, finely minced

3 eggs

2 tablespoons olive oil (butter can also be used)

¼ teaspoon turmeric

¼ teaspoon sea salt

1 tablespoon fresh or 1½ teaspoons dried oregano

1 cup grated goat cheese

¼ cup whole grain oat flour or whole grain bread crumbs

## instructions

Preheat oven to 350°F. In oven-to-table cookware, whisk eggs and goat cheese together, then add remaining ingredients, making sure to mix thoroughly. Sprinkle with extra dried oregano just before placing in the oven. Bake 20 to 25 minutes, or until the center of the frittata is set and top is lightly golden. Cool to room temperature. Just before serving, sprinkle with fresh wheat grass and/or parsley. Store in fridge or freezer.

CAN ALSO BE SERVED RAW

*Simply delete the flour or bread crumbs or replace with cooked rice, oatmeal or grated raw sweet potato. Blend all ingredients and serve.*

*The benefits of artichoke hearts:*

An antioxidant super food, artichoke hearts contain a variety of phytonutrients that have anti-cancer qualities, and also support the immune system. Excellent source of vitamin C and some of the most powerful polyphenol-type antioxidants, including quercetin, rutin, anthocyanins and silymarin.

# simple fruit'n oats with homemade *yogurt*

*Make this tasty breakfast dish the night before so the oats have a chance to soften.*

## ingredients

$1/2$ cup rolled oats

8 ounces homemade yogurt (or yogurt from the store – without sugar or artificial sweeteners – if you don't wish to make your own)

$1/4$ cup fresh fruit
(e.g., bananas, blueberries, strawberries)

## instructions

Put rolled oats in a bowl. Add yogurt and fruit and mix well. Soak overnight in the refrigerator and serve at room temperature in the morning.

For extra pizzazz, add some simple granola (no salt or sugar) just before serving. Homemade yogurt can be stored in containers in the refrigerator. It will last as long as commercial brands.

### *Homemade yogurt*

To make your own yogurt, boil 1 liter of whole milk (goat milk can also be used) for 15 minutes, making sure it does not burn. Watch the milk very carefully. Turn the heat down before it reaches a rolling boil. Let the milk cool until it is lukewarm.

In a small mixing bowl, combine one 175g container of yogurt with a small amount of the milk, until it is smooth. Return to the pot and leave it until yogurt has formed. This can take 8 to 12 hours.

*The benefits of strawberries:*
Considered one of the world's healthiest foods, strawberries contain an amazing combination of phytonutrients, including anthocyanins, ellagitannins, flavonols, terpenoids, and phenolic acids.

page 69
roaring raita with parsley

# toppers

# stock that *rocks*

*This gives you a nutrient-dense broth to add to any recipe, including biscuits and treats, or as a topper for regular meals.*

## ingredients

24 cups filtered water

3 pounds chicken backs and necks

2 carrots, in pieces

2 celery stalks, in pieces

3 Shiitake mushrooms, dried or fresh

2 cloves garlic

1" piece fresh ginger, minced

12 white peppercorns

1 to 2 tablespoons Kosher salt, to taste

Handful fresh parsley, Italian or curly

Other fresh herbs to taste (e.g., thyme, oregano, sage, rosemary)

## instructions

Put all ingredients in a large stockpot. Bring to a rolling boil, skim off the foam, turn the heat down to simmer, and leave the pot to sit and stew all day. Refrigerate overnight.

Next morning, skim off the fat, remove the meat and vegetables (which you can give to your dog - make sure all the cooked bones are removed), strain the stock into storage containers, and freeze.

*The benefits of celery:*

A surprise package of nutrients and anti-inflammatory properties, celery contains a unique polysaccharide called apiuman, along with vitamin C, beta-carotene, and manganese. The phytonutrients found in celery have been shown to help prevent inflammatory reactions in the digestive tract and blood vessels.

# mushroom medley

*This tasty, protein-packed recipe will tempt even the pickiest palate.*

## ingredients

1 cup beef strips

1 cup liver (e.g., beef, chicken, turkey), cut into bite size pieces

1 cup Shiitake mushrooms, finely chopped or sliced
(if using dried, this is the volume after rehydration)

1 cup Shiitake tea*

1 cup zucchini, chopped

1" piece fresh ginger finely minced, or 1 teaspoon ground ginger

2 to 3 cloves garlic, finely minced

½ teaspoon sea salt

1 cup filtered water or broth

1 tablespoon olive oil

## instructions

Combine all ingredients in a large pot. Bring to a boil, then turn down heat to simmer. Simmer gently until there is no pink in the meat. Remove from stove and cool.

Serve as an addition/topping to your dog's regular meals. This recipe can also be served with rice.

note: **To make Shiitake tea, break up two dried Shiitake mushrooms into small pieces and place them in 1 cup of filtered water in a small pot. Bring to a boil, then reduce the heat to simmer for 30 minutes. Strain mushroom bits and cool tea. Mushroom pieces can also be added to your dog's meal.*

CAN ALSO BE SERVED RAW

*Grate, finely chop or purée zucchini and mushrooms and mix with raw beef, liver and other ingredients.*

*The benefits of olive oil:*

Olive oil has been called "the ancient giver of life," and next to salt, it is considered the "essence of civilization." Olive oil is a very rich source of vitamins A and E, helping to neutralize cancer causing free radicals. It is also rich in Omega-9 Oleic acid, a mono-saturated fat that helps to protect the heart and also supports skin health. When you purchase olive oil, ensure that the label says "extra virgin" which means that the oil has come from the first pressing of the olives, with less than 1% acidity, and it has the most health benefits and the best taste.

CAN ALSO BE SERVED RAW

# winter sun carrot and apple soup

*Naturally sweet and delicious, your dog will love slurping up this one!*

## ingredients

1 cup chicken or vegetable stock

2 cups pureed carrots (with peel), or try sweet potato, yams, squash or pumpkin

1 cup pureed red apples

1 tablespoon olive oil

1 teaspoon sea salt

1½ teaspoons cinnamon

¼ teaspoon ginger

## instructions

This soup can be served raw or cooked. For raw soup, simply combine all ingredients and add a tablespoon or two to your dog's regular meals. You can also freeze this delicious and nutritious soup in ice cube trays for treats and meal fixings.

For cooked soup, combine all ingredients in a medium sized pot. Bring to a boil. As soon as you see bubbles forming on the surface, turn down the heat and simmer gently for 30 minutes. Cool soup to room temperature before serving to your dog or adding to his regular food.

*The benefits of carrots:*

No wonder Bugs loved them! Carrots contain beta carotene, vitamins B, C, D, E and K, riboflavin, niacin, calcium, potassium, phosphorus, iron, magnesium, manganese and iodine. They support the immune system, aid digestion, and are recognized as a glandular tonic.

# roaring raita with parsley

*Great for the warm weather, this topper is chock full of nutritious herbs.*

## ingredients

1 cup fresh parsley

1/4 to 1/2 cup fresh mint leaves

1½ teaspoons grated fresh ginger

1 clove garlic, minced

1/4 teaspoon sea salt

1½ teaspoons lemon juice (optional)

1/4 cup yogurt (without sugar or artificial sweeteners)

## instructions

This dish can be prepared by hand or in a food processor or blender. Combine everything except the yogurt. Transfer to a bowl, stir in yogurt, then cover and refrigerate until serving. This recipe makes a great meal topper for your canine companion. It is very refreshing in hot weather. Try freezing it in ice cube trays. This is a recipe that the whole family can share.

See photo page 64

*The benefits of mint:*
No wonder mint tea is so good after a big meal! Mint is a digestive carminative and is soothing to the digestive system. It's also a good source of potassium and magnesium.

# savory *soup* with apples and sweet potatoes

*What a yummy way to serve veggies and fruit!*

## ingredients

1 cup chicken or vegetable stock

2 cups puréed sweet potatoes, yams or squash

1 cup puréed red apples

1 tablespoon olive oil

1 teaspoon sea salt (optional)

1 teaspoon cinnamon powder

¼ teaspoon ground ginger

CAN ALSO BE SERVED RAW

## instructions

This soup can be served raw or cooked and can be added to regular meals as a sauce or garnish.

*cooked*: Combine all ingredients in a saucepan. Bring to a boil. Turn down heat and simmer gently for 30 minutes. Cool soup completely before serving to your dog.

*raw*: Combine all ingredients, and add a tablespoon or two to regular meals.

*frozen:* Freeze in ice cube trays for treats and meal fixings.

*The benefits of squash:*

Tasty and super healthy, summer and winter squash are packed with antioxidants that keep free radicals at bay, and offer anti-inflammatory benefits too.

# liver paté

*A nutritious, high-protein topper to tempt even the most finicky of appetites.*

CAN ALSO BE SERVED RAW

## ingredients

½ pound liver, e.g., chicken, bison

2 eggs

1 teaspoon sea salt or kelp

1 tablespoon first pressed olive oil

## instructions

For raw paté: whirl ingredients together in a food processor or blender, until smooth. Store in an airtight container in the refrigerator, and use as a topper for regular meals.

For cooked paté: hard boil the eggs and set aside. Lightly sauté liver in a pan with the olive oil, sea salt and kelp. Cook until there is no pink left. Allow to cool and then combine all ingredients in a food processor or blender until smooth, and serve and store as above.

*The benefits of liver:*

Liver from grass fed animals is a rich source of nutrients, including calcium, phosphorus, magnesium, potassium, iron, zinc, copper, vitamins A, B6, B12, C, D, and E, thiamin, riboflavin, niacin, pantothenic acid, folic acid, and biotin.

cancer cookies
page 79

# special *needs*

# buffalo sauté

*High in protein, low in fat... this is one the whole family can enjoy.*

## ingredients

1 pound buffalo, sliced into strips

4 tablespoons extra virgin olive oil

1 clove garlic, finely minced, or
1/2 teaspoon granulated garlic

1 teaspoon sea salt

2 teaspoons rubbed oregano

1 teaspoon thyme

1 teaspoon dried parsley

1/2 teaspoon cinnamon

1/2 teaspoon nutmeg

1 cup grated sweet potato

1 cup grated yam

6 tablespoons filtered water

Greek yogurt for garnish

## instructions

Place olive oil in a large pan. Turn heat to high. When you see the first bubbles appear on the surface of the oil, add the sliced buffalo strips. Turn down the heat to simmer. Add all spices. Using a wooden spoon, gently turn pieces of buffalo until all the pink is gone. Remove pan from the stove. Allow the buffalo strips to cool, and then remove to a plate or bowl.

You should be left with a beautiful golden sauce. Take your grated sweet potato and yam and add it to the pan along with the filtered water. Turn the heat to medium high, and gently combine all ingredients together. As soon as bubbles appear, turn the heat down to simmer, cover your pan, and allow to simmer for 15 minutes. Remove the pan from the stove and let it cool.

Serve this dish at room temperature to your dog (serve hot for human family members), and add a dollop of Greek or goat yogurt just before serving.

CAN ALSO BE SERVED RAW

*Just blend together all the ingredients and serve.*

### About buffalo:

Bison/buffalo is considered a "non-allergenic" protein, making it an excellent choice for companion animals that have a sensitivity or allergy to red meat. Grass fed bison contains no pesticides, herbicides, hormones, or antibiotics. It has a much higher protein content than beef, but is much lower in fat. Buffalo is a nutrient-dense food that is an excellent source of Omega-3 fatty acids. It is high in CLA (Conjugated Linolenic Acid), which helps to block tumor growth, and is helpful as part of a weight reduction progamme.

# duck with quinoa

*Another alternative protein, duck makes a great meal for dogs with allergies.*

## ingredients

2 pounds duck, e.g., legs

1/2 cup (6 to 8) dried Shiitake mushrooms

3 strips Kombu kelp

½" to 1" piece fresh ginger, minced

2 star anise

1 teaspoon sea salt

5 cups filtered water

1 cup quinoa

## instructions

Combine all ingredients except quinoa in a big pot. As soon as you have a rolling boil, turn heat down to a medium simmer, and continue to simmer until the duck meat begins to fall off the bone. Don't worry about watching the pot. Leave it for 1½ to 2 hours. Then remove the meat from the bones, and return meat to the pot. Discard the bones.

Take 1 cup quinoa, put it in a strainer and rinse well under filtered water. Put in a small pot and add 1¼ cups filtered water. Turn heat to high. As soon as bubbles appear, turn heat down to simmer, put a lid on the pot, and time for 12 minutes. Turn heat off. Using a fork, "fluff" the quinoa then leave it for five minutes. Serve at room temperature.

This dish can also be served with Thai jasmine rice, which is wonderful for gastrointestinal problems. It is so easy to add this to your duck dish, once you have removed the meat from the bones. Simply add 1 cup of rice to the pot, and simmer for approximately 20 minutes, until the water has been absorbed.

### The benefits of star anise:

A culinary spice and medicinal herb cultivated from an evergreen tree native to areas of China and Vietnam, star anise is most widely used in the treatment of digestive ailments. Star anise activates the body's digestive enzymes, aiding in the digestion of meat and fats. It also helps speed up the healing process, has antibacterial properties, and helps discourage the growth of yeast and fungus.

# awesome *allergy* treats

*Your dog has allergies, but she still loves variety! Let the ingredients below inspire you to create the perfect treat. This diet is based on an elimination diet.*

## ingredients

2 cups puréed protein source (e.g. venison, rabbit, turkey, mutton, ostrich, bison or emu)

2 cups whole grain flour (e.g. brown rice, amaranth, quinoa, potato)

½ cup filtered water

hint: *In an elimination diet, try using one protein only for two weeks. If your dog continues to show allergy symptoms, try a different protein. If she experiences no reaction, she can tolerate this protein.*

## instructions

Preheat oven to 325°F. Cover a cookie sheet with parchment paper. Place the meat and filtered water in a food processor or blender, and whirl until smooth. Add flour a little at a time, so it is well incorporated into the meat. The dough will be a bit sticky.

Turn dough out onto a well floured board or counter. Make small balls of dough, roll in flour, then roll out the dough as you would clay, making pencil shapes that are as small or large as you like, depending on the size of your dog. Take a sharp knife and cut treats, then place them on the cookie sheet.

Bake for 30 minutes, then turn down oven to 175°F and bake for another 30 minutes. Turn off oven and allow treats to cool completely before removing them from the oven and storing them in a Ziploc bag or container in the fridge.

*The benefits of amaranth:*
Made from the seed of the amaranth plant, it's high in protein and a good source of lysine.

# *exotic* eats

*Another tasty dish for the whole family! If your dog is not allergic, you can serve it with rice.*

## ingredients

1 pound ostrich, emu, bison, venison, rabbit or duck, ground

3 tablespoons extra virgin olive oil

1 small garlic clove, minced, or ¼ teaspoon granulated garlic

½ teaspoon sea salt

1 tablespoon rubbed oregano

2 cups tomatoes, diced, or 1 can tomatoes, with juice.

## instructions

Place extra virgin olive oil in pan. Turn heat to medium. Add ground meat. Gently mix with the olive oil, and add garlic and oregano, continuing to stir. As soon as bubbles appear, turn down heat to simmer, and continue to stir until there is no pink remaining in the meat.

Add the tomatoes, and combine thoroughly. Put a lid on the pan and simmer for 20 minutes.

Cool to room temperature before serving.

CAN ALSO BE SERVED RAW

*Simply mix all the ingredients together and serve*

*The benefits of emu:*

Both emu and ostrich are good protein alternatives for dogs with allergies. Emu is a valuable source of thiamin, riboflavin, iron, zinc, phosphorus, magnesium, vitamins B6 and B12, pantothenic acid, selenium, and even, vitamin C.

# liver broth and purée

*This recipe packs a healthy punch of B vitamins and is good for cancer patients.*

## ingredients

½ to 1 pound chicken or beef liver, or other liver of your choice

Filtered water

1 clove garlic

## instructions

Put liver in a medium sized pot and cover with filtered water. Add peeled clove of garlic. Bring to a rapid boil, then turn down to simmer. Remove from heat as soon as no pink is seen in the liver. Cool, pour off broth, then whirl liver in a food processor or blender. Add a little dollop of broth or purée to your animal's daily meals for extra taste and nutrition. For even more zip, add a teaspoon of oregano to the mix.

See photo page 80

*Why filtered water?*

Water borne contaminants can cause a variety of health issues. Sources suggest that using a water filtration system can remove up to 2,100 known toxins.

# cancer cookies

*When they don't really feel like eating, tempt them with these simple tasty treats.*

## ingredients

4½ cups chickpea flour

1 cup applesauce

2 teaspoons cinnamon

2 teaspoons carob powder

## instructions

Preheat oven to 325°F. Combine ingredients in a food processor. Cover a large cookie sheet with parchment paper. Turn out dough onto a lightly floured surface and knead well. Cut into desired shapes, or take small pieces of dough, roll out to pencil thickness and cut pieces appropriate to your dog's size (using a knife dipped in hot water). Place on cookie sheet and bake for 20 minutes, then turn oven down to 175°F and allow cookies to bake for 40 more minutes. Turn oven off and allow cookies to cool before removing them. Store in an airtight container or Ziploc bag.

This recipe is easily adapted to meet the changing tastes of your dog. You can replace the applesauce with organic canned pumpkin or banana, or replace with puréed liver and use 1 finely minced garlic clove and 2 teaspoons fresh parsley in place of the cinnamon and carob powder.

See photo page 72

### The benefits of applesauce:

Often recommended for mild cases of diarrhea, applesauce can be added to food or used on its own. It contains pectin, a natural fibrous substance, which acts to tighten bowels, although it takes time to work. Generally, you can expect a solidified stool within three days.

page 84
Vee Vee's remedy for IBD

page 78
liver broth and purée

slippery elm and honey gruel
page 82

# slippery elm and honey gruel

*Gruels containing slippery elm and honey are an internal salve for all kinds of digestive problems. Slippery elm is also used in the original Essiac, an herbal formula developed to fight cancer.*

## ingredients

1 cup slippery elm bark powder

1/2 cup oat flakes

1/2 cup barley flakes

1/4 cup arrowroot

1 tablespoon marshmallow (*Althea officinalis*)

1 tablespoon wheat germ

1 tablespoon dill seed

1 teaspoon unpasteurized honey

1 cup yogurt (without sugar or artificial sweeteners)

Filtered warm water

## instructions

Combine the slippery elm powder mix, oat flakes, barley flakes, arrowroot, marshmallow, wheat germ and dill seed. Store in an airtight container. When you want to make a "batch" of gruel, see below.

### gruel

Take 1 teaspoon of this mixture and combine it with the unpasteurized honey. Ensure that ingredients are thoroughly blended.

Whisk in a little filtered warm water, e.g. 1 tablespoon to begin with, along with the goat milk yogurt. Add more water if needed.

### puppies and small dogs

1 to 1½ teaspoons added to each meal

### medium dogs

1 tablespoon added to each meal

### large dogs

1½ tablespoons added to each meal

note: *The gruel recipe above makes enough gruel for several days' worth of meals.*

See photo page 81

### The benefits of slippery elm bark:

Juliette de Bairacli Levy, the grandmother of the herbal movement, called it simply "tree bark's flour." It's made from the slippery elm tree. This nutrient dense food coats and heals inflamed tissue, internally and externally. It soothes the gastrointestinal tract and protects the lungs too. Slippery elm is a great food for puppies, senior dogs, and dogs who are very weak so it's perfect for convalescence.

# the *potato* diet

*This is a modified version of a time-tested recipe from holistic veterinarian Dr. Martin Goldstein's* The Nature of Animal Healing. *It is excellent for dogs with gastrointestinal upsets such as chronic diarrhea.*

## ingredients

50% white potatoes

50% sweet potatoes

Slice of turnip

## instructions

Boil all the ingredients together and then mix with boiled chicken or lamb for flavor.

*The benefits of turnip:*

Rich in nutrition, turnips are an excellent source of calcium and potassium, and high in fiber. They also contain vitamins A, C, and E, manganese, and beta-carotene. Turnip greens are a valuable source of vitamin K and Omega 3 fatty acids.

# Vee Vee's *remedy* for IBD

*Inflammatory bowel disease is a difficult-to-treat affliction that can result in diarrhea, vomiting, malabsorption, weight loss, painful bowel movements and abdominal swelling. This recipe helped a golden retriever named Vee Vee recover. It's also good for dogs with pancreatitis and colitis.*

## ingredients

4 cups oat flour

1 cup oatmeal

1 cup oat bran

2 teaspoons cinnamon

2 tablespoons Manuka honey

2 tablespoons molasses

2 cups unsweetened applesauce

## instructions

Preheat oven to 350 F. Combine all ingredients in a food processor or mixer – the dough is ready when it pulls away from the sides of the bowl. Turn it out onto a floured cutting board and knead a few times. If you find the dough is too wet, add more oat flour. Take small pieces of the dough and roll out to a thickness of about ¼". Cut into desired shapes or score into squares with a knife. You can also roll out the dough to pencil thickness and cut into small pieces.

Place biscuits on lightly greased cookie sheets or parchment paper. You should have sufficient dough to fill 2 cookie sheets. If you like, you can make 1 sheet of biscuits, and freeze the remainder for another time. Bake for 20 minutes. Turn off the oven, and let the biscuits completely cool before removing them. You can leave the biscuits in an open bowl, where they will continue to harden, or store in a Ziploc bag or cookie jar.

As an alternative to biscuits, you can make mini muffins using the same recipe with the addition of 1 teaspoon of baking soda and 1 teaspoon of baking powder. Fill mini muffin cups and baking for 15 minutes.

note: *You can also make mini muffins for your canine companion (and yourself), by adding 1 teaspoon baking soda and 1 teaspoon gluten free baking powder to the recipe, though these ingredients are optional. Fill each mini muffin cup. Bake 15 minutes in the preheated oven. Your dog will love you!*

### *The benefits of oat bran:*

Oat bran contains a special type of fiber called beta-glucan, shown to lower cholesterol, which helps to reduce the risk of heart disease, and support the immune system's response to bacterial infections, viruses, fungi, and parasites. Beta-glucans also help to stabilize blood sugar levels and inhibit the the growth of tumors, as well as contribute to reducing the risk of some cancers.

See photo page 80

# gluten *free* truffles

*Now even dogs with gluten sensitivities can indulge!*

## ingredients

3 cups whole brown rice flakes

1 cup whole quinoa flour or 1/2 cup whole quinoa flour and 1/2 cup coconut flour (hemp, almond and chickpea flours can also be used)

1/2 cup hemp butter or apple butter (almond or pumpkin butter can also be used or try a combination)

1 tablespoon cinnamon

1/2 teaspoon ginger powder

1 tablespoon carob powder

1/2 cup filtered water

Oatmeal for rolling

## instructions

Preheat oven to 325°F. Cover one large cookie sheet with parchment paper. Combine all ingredients in a food processor, mixer or by hand.

Using a measuring spoon, shape perfectly sized truffles. Roll in oatmeal and place on cookie sheet. Bake for 20 minutes.

Remove from oven and cool completely before storing in Ziploc bags. This recipe can easily be doubled or tripled and freezes beautifully.

*The benefits of quinoa:*

Quinoa, technically considered a "pseudo-grain," is usually included alongside the true cereal grains, because its nutritional profile, preparation, and use are so similar. Quinoa is actually an amino acid packed protein seed, related to beets, chard, and spinach. It is considered a whole protein because it contains all nine essential amino acids, including lysine, which is crucial to tissue growth and repair. Quinoa is perfect for gluten free diets.

# treats *without* sweets

*This recipe is ideal for diabetic dogs.*

## ingredients

3 cups barley flakes

1/2 cup hemp flour

1/2 cup hemp hearts

2 tablespoons unsweetened coconut

1 tablespoon dried cranberries, finely minced

2 teaspoons pumpkin spice (a combination of cinnamon and allspice)

2 teaspoons cinnamon

1/4 cup hemp seed oil

1 1/2 cups applesauce (1/2 cup of applesauce can be replaced with 1/2 cup carrot purée or apple butter.)

Kelp

## instructions

Cover a large cookie sheet with parchment paper. Combine all ingredients in a processor or mixer, or by hand. Roll out dough and cut into desired shapes, or spread out on cookie sheet and lightly score.

Sprinkle with kelp before placing in a "cold" oven. Turn oven to 350°F. When it reaches this heat, turn down to 250°F and leave biscuits to bake for approximately 45 more minutes. Every oven is different, so check your biscuits; they should be deep golden in color with no burnt edges.

Turn oven off and allow the biscuits to cool completely before storing them in an open container or in a Ziploc bag or cookie jar. This recipe makes over 5 dozen large round biscuits.

This recipe can easily be doubled or tripled, and stores perfectly in the freezer.

*The benefits of hemp flour:*
An excellent source of fiber and protein, hemp flour also contains Omega 3 and Omega 6 essential fatty acids.

# kidney cookies

*These treats are a healthful option for canine kidney patients.*

## ingredients

2½ cups whole grain flour
(spelt, brown rice, barley, etc.)

½ teaspoon garlic powder or
1 fresh clove garlic, finely minced

½ cup chicken broth
(or other low sodium canned broth)

½ cup filtered water

1 cup puréed green beans and carrots
(or zucchini, parsley, celery, dandelion greens, collard greens, squash and/or turnip)

## instructions

Preheat oven to 350°F. Whirl together ingredients in a blender or food processor until well incorporated. Turn the dough onto a floured board and knead a few times. Roll it out and cut into desired shapes, or place the dough on a lightly greased or parchment paper covered cookie sheet, roll it out to the corners of the sheet and lightly score it with a knife.

Bake for 25 minutes. Turn the oven off, and let the treats cool completely in the oven. Remove and store in a Ziploc bag or cookie jar.

*The benefits of dandelion greens:*
Dandelion greens are packed with vitamins and minerals, including calcium and iron, vitamin C, some of the B vitamins, vitamin E, and vitamin K. They even contain more protein than spinach.

# index